PERFECT RISOTTO

Consultant Editor:
Valerie Ferguson

LORENZ BOOKS

Contents

Introduction

Risotto, the rich, creamy and comforting creation of Milan in the 16th century, is the most famous of all Italian rice dishes. Traditionally it is made with the finest arborio or carnaroli rice. All risottos are prepared basically in the same way, although they can be flavoured with an almost endless variety of ingredients. The rice is coated in butter or oil, then simmering stock is added, one ladleful at a time, and the rice is gently stirred over a low heat until all the liquid has been completely absorbed. Only then is more stock added, and the risotto is cooked in this way for about 20-30 minutes, until the rice is tender, moist and creamy but retaining a little "bite".

A number of the vegetable risottos in this book can be made vegetarian by using a vegetable stock where a chicken or meat stock is specified. Several recipes are included which call for brown rice – for example, Chicken and Bean Risotto – but arborio or carnaroli rice could be substituted, if preferred, and more stock used.

The recipes in this inspiring collection reflect the versatility of risottos, from light lunches, main meals and accompaniments to moulds and stuffings for vegetables, using a wide variety of ingredients and seasonings to bring you the authentic taste of Italy.

Rice

The Saracens first introduced rice to Italy as long ago as the 11th century (some believe even earlier), but it became popular only in the 16th century, when it began to be cultivated on a large scale in the Po Valley in Piedmont. Traditionally, rice has played a much greater part in the cooking of northern Italy than in the south, particularly in the Veneto, where the famous dish of *risi e bisi* (Venetian dialect for "rice and peas") opened the banquet served every year by the Doges to honour their patron saint, Mark.

Carnaroli

Superfino carnaroli

The finest quality short-grain rice, known as superfino carnaroli, is preferred for risotto. It swells to at least three times its original size during cooking, enabling it to absorb all the cooking liquid while still retaining its shape and firm, *al dente* texture combined with a creamy smoothness.

Also highly prized as a perfect rice for risotto, vialone nano is less easy to buy outside Italy. It can sometimes be found in specialist delicatessens.

Vialone nano

Today, Italy produces more rice, in greater variety, than anywhere else in Europe. Most of it is grown in the Po Valley, where conditions are perfect for cultivating the shortgrain carnaroli and arborio rice, which make the best risotto and can now be found in many supermarkets.

Superfino arborio

Arborio

COOK'S TIP: If you are unable to find arborio or carnaroli rice, use the best quality roundgrain rice you have available.

Stock

Good-quality stock is essential for a risotto and it is worth the effort to prepare it at home. Home-made stock may be frozen successfully for several months.

FISH STOCK

INGREDIENTS
1 onion
1 carrot
1 celery stick
any fish bones, skin and trimmings available
6 black peppercorns
2 bay leaves
3 fresh parsley sprigs

1 Peel and coarsely slice the onion. Peel and chop the carrot, and scrub and slice the celery.

2 Place all the ingredients in a large saucepan and add enough water to cover. Bring to the boil, skim the surface and simmer, uncovered, for 20 minutes. Strain and use the stock immediately or store for up to 2 days in the fridge.

BROWN STOCK

INGREDIENTS
30 ml/2 tbsp vegetable oil
1.5 kg/3–3½ lb shin, shank or neck of
  beef bones, cut into pieces
225 g/8 oz shin of beef, cut
  into pieces
1 bouquet garni
2 onions, trimmed and quartered
2 carrots, scrubbed and chopped
2 celery sticks, sliced
5 ml/1 tsp black peppercorns
2.5 ml/½ tsp salt

1 Preheat the oven to 220°C/425°F/ Gas 7. Drizzle the vegetable oil over the bottom of a roasting tin and add the bones and meat. Coat in the oil and bake for 25–30 minutes, or until well browned, turning regularly during cooking to ensure even browning.

2 Transfer the meat and bones to a large saucepan, add the remaining ingredients and cover with 3.2 litres/ 5½ pints/14 cups water. Bring to the boil, skim the surface, then partially cover and simmer for 2½–3 hours, or until reduced to 1.75 litres/3 pints/ 7½ cups. Strain and cool; remove the solidified fat before use. Store for up to 4 days in the fridge.

CHICKEN OR WHITE STOCK

INGREDIENTS
1 onion
4 cloves
1 carrot
2 leeks
2 celery sticks
1 cooked or raw chicken carcass or 675 g/
    1½ lb veal bones, cut into pieces
1 bouquet garni
8 black peppercorns
2.5 ml/½ tsp salt

VEGETABLE STOCK

INGREDIENTS
1 onion
2 carrots
2 large celery sticks, plus small amounts of
    any of the following: leeks, celeriac,
    parsnip, turnip, cabbage or cauliflower
    trimmings, mushroom peelings
30 ml/2 tbsp vegetable oil
1 bouquet garni
6 black peppercorns

1 Peel the onion, cut into quarters and spike each quarter with a clove. Scrub and roughly chop the remaining vegetables. Place the vegetables in a large saucepan with the remaining ingredients.

2 Cover with 1.75 litres/3 pints/ 7½ cups water. Bring to the boil, skim the surface and simmer, partially covered, for 2 hours. Strain and allow to cool. When cold, remove the hardened fat before using. Store for up to 4 days in the fridge.

1 Peel and slice the onion. Scrub and roughly chop the remaining vegetables. Heat the oil in a large pan and fry all the vegetables until soft and lightly browned. Add the remaining ingredients and cover with 1.75 litres/ 3 pints/7½ cups water.

2 Bring to the boil, skim the surface, then partially cover and simmer for 1½ hours. Strain and allow to cool. Store the stock in the fridge for up to 3 days.

Making Risotto

Risotto lends itself to many variations and, depending on the flavourings and additions, it can be served as a first course, a main dish or an accompaniment. For best results use well-flavoured home-made stock.

1 In a saucepan, bring the measured quantity of stock to the boil, then reduce the heat so the liquid is kept at a gentle simmer.

3 Add the rice and stir to coat it with the fat. Sauté for 1–2 minutes over a moderate heat, stirring.

2 Heat butter, oil or a mixture of the two in a wide, heavy pan. Add chopped onion (plus garlic and/or other flavourings specified in the recipe) and cook over a low heat until soft, stirring occasionally.

4 Add a little of the simmering stock (or an initial quantity of wine or vermouth, if specified in the recipe) and stir well. Simmer, stirring frequently, until the rice has absorbed almost all of the liquid. The risotto should bubble but not boil fiercely.

5 Add some more of the simmering stock and cook, stirring, until it is almost all absorbed. Continue adding the stock in this way until the grains of rice are tender but still firm to the bite (*al dente*, like pasta) and the risotto is creamy but not runny. Use smaller quantities of stock towards the end of cooking. The risotto will take about 30 minutes to cook in total.

Salmon Risotto with Cucumber & Tarragon

Fresh tarragon and cucumber bring out the flavour of the salmon.

Serves 4

INGREDIENTS
25 g/1 oz/2 tbsp butter
1 small bunch spring onions, white part only, chopped
½ cucumber, peeled, seeded and chopped
400 g/14 oz/2 cups arborio or carnaroli rice
900 ml/1½ pints/3¾ cups simmering fish or chicken stock
150 ml/¼ pint/⅔ cup dry white wine
450 g/1 lb salmon fillet, skinned and diced
45ml/3 tbsp chopped fresh tarragon

1 Heat the butter in a large saucepan and add the spring onions and cucumber. Cook for 2–3 minutes without colouring.

2 Add the rice, stock and wine, bring to the boil and simmer, uncovered, for 10 minutes, stirring occasionally.

3 Stir in the diced salmon and tarragon. Continue cooking for a further 5 minutes, then switch off the heat. Cover and leave to stand for 5 minutes before serving.

Risotto with Prawns

This risotto is given a soft pink colour to complement the prawns by the addition of a little tomato purée.

Serves 4

INGREDIENTS
350g/12 oz raw prawns in their shells
1 bay leaf
1–2 fresh parsley sprigs
5 ml/1 tsp whole black peppercorns
2 garlic cloves, peeled
1.2 litres/2 pints/5 cups water
65 g/2½ oz/5 tbsp butter
2 shallots, finely chopped
275 g/10 oz/1½ cups arborio or carnaroli rice
15 ml/1 tbsp tomato purée softened in
    120 ml/4 fl oz/½ cup dry white wine
salt and freshly ground black pepper

1 Simmer the first 5 ingredients in the water for 4 minutes. Strain, reserving the liquid and allow to cool.

2 Peel the prawns and boil the shells only for another 10 minutes. Strain and simmer until needed.

3 Slice the prawns in half lengthways, removing the dark vein along the back. Set 4 halves aside for the garnish and roughly chop the rest.

4 Heat two-thirds of the butter, add the shallots and cook until golden. Stir in the prawns; cook for 1–2 minutes. Add the rice, mixing well, and after 1–2 minutes pour in the tomato purée and wine. Add the hot stock gradually, following steps 4–5 for Making Risotto. Add the remaining butter and season to taste. Serve with the reserved prawn halves.

Lobster & Truffle Risotto

Luxurious lobster and fabulous fresh truffle are partnered in this silky-smooth risotto. Both truffle shavings and truffle oil are added towards the end of cooking to preserve their flavour.

Serves 4

INGREDIENTS
50 g/2 oz/4 tbsp unsalted butter
1 medium onion, chopped
400 g/14 oz/2 cups arborio or carnaroli rice
1 fresh thyme sprig
1.2 litres/2 pints/5 cups simmering
   chicken stock
150 ml/¼ pint/⅔ cup dry white wine
1 freshly cooked lobster
45 ml/3 tbsp chopped fresh parsley and chervil
3–4 drops truffle oil
2 hard-boiled eggs, sliced
1 fresh black or white truffle
fresh parsley sprigs, to garnish

2 Twist off the lobster tail, cut the underside with scissors and remove the white tail meat. Slice half of the meat, then roughly chop the remainder. Break open the claws with a small hammer and remove the flesh, in one piece if possible.

3 Remove the rice from the heat, stir in the chopped lobster meat, chopped herbs and truffle oil. Cover and leave to stand for 5 minutes.

4 Divide among warmed dishes and arrange the remaining lobster, hard-boiled egg slices and shavings of fresh truffle on top. Garnish with parsley and serve.

1 Melt the butter in a large, shallow pan, add the onion and fry gently until soft but not coloured. Add the rice and thyme sprig and stir well to coat evenly with fat. Pour in the chicken stock and wine, stir once, bring to a simmer and cook, uncovered, for 15 minutes.

COOK'S TIP: To make the most of the aromatic truffle scent, keep the tuber in the rice jar for a few days. Alternatively, store with the raw eggs at room temperature.

Seafood Risotto

Revive memories of Mediterranean holidays with this dish, a showcase for glorious seafood.

Serves 4

INGREDIENTS
60 ml/4 tbsp sunflower oil
1 onion, chopped
2 garlic cloves, crushed
225 g/8 oz/generous 1 cup arborio or
    carnaroli rice
105 ml/7 tbsp white wine
1.5 litres/2½ pints/6¼ cups simmering
    fish stock
350 g/12 oz mixed seafood, such as raw
    prawns, mussels, squid rings and clams
grated rind of ½ lemon
30 ml/2 tbsp tomato purée
15 ml/1 tbsp chopped fresh parsley
salt and freshly ground black pepper

2 Add the hot stock gradually and simmer, stirring frequently, following steps 4–5 for Making Risotto.

3 After about 10 minutes, stir in the seafood and cook for 2–3 minutes. Continue to add hot stock until the rice is cooked. Use less stock towards the end of cooking so that the risotto is creamy and not runny.

4 Stir in the lemon rind, tomato purée and parsley. Season with salt and pepper and serve warm.

1 Heat the oil in a heavy-based pan, add the onion and garlic and cook until soft. Add the rice and stir to coat the grains with oil. Add the wine and cook over a moderate heat, stirring, for a few minutes, until absorbed.

COOK'S TIP: During cooking, adjust the heat so that the risotto bubbles steadily, but don't let it boil fiercely or the stock will evaporate before it can be absorbed by the rice.

Shellfish Risotto with Fruits of the Forest

Distinctive but subtle-tasting wild mushrooms complement the mild flavours of fresh shellfish.

Serves 4

INGREDIENTS
45 ml/3 tbsp olive oil
1 medium onion, chopped
225 g/8 oz/generous 3 cups assorted wild
    and cultivated mushrooms, trimmed
    and sliced
450 g/1 lb/2¼ cups arborio or carnaroli rice
1.2 litres/2 pints/5 cups simmering chicken
    or vegetable stock
150 ml/¼ pint/⅔ cup white wine
115 g/4 oz raw prawns, heads removed
225 g/8 oz live mussels, beards removed
225 g/8 oz Venus or carpet shell clams
1 medium squid, cleaned, trimmed and sliced
3 drops truffle oil (optional)
75 ml/5 tbsp chopped fresh parsley
    and chervil
celery salt and cayenne pepper

1 Heat the oil in a large frying pan and fry the onion for 6–8 minutes, until soft but not brown.

2 Add the mushrooms and soften until their juices begin to run. Stir in the rice and heat through.

3 Pour in the stock and wine. Add the prawns, mussels, clams and squid, stir and simmer for 15 minutes.

4 Add the truffle oil if using, stir in the herbs, cover and stand for 5–10 minutes. Season to taste with celery salt and a pinch of cayenne pepper and serve immediately.

COOK'S TIP: Before cooking, scrub the mussels and clams, then tap them with a knife. If any of the shells do not close, discard them. After cooking (see step 3), if any of the shells have not opened, discard them as well.

Chicken & Vegetable Risotto

A colourful risotto combining red and yellow peppers, green beans and mushrooms with minced chicken.

Serves 4

INGREDIENTS
15 ml/1 tbsp oil
200 g/7 oz/1 cup arborio or
    carnaroli rice
1 onion, chopped
225 g/8 oz/2 cups uncooked minced chicken
600 ml/1 pint/2½ cups simmering
    chicken stock
1 red pepper, seeded and chopped
1 yellow pepper, seeded and chopped
75 g/3 oz frozen green beans, thawed
115 g/4 oz/scant 2 cups chestnut
    mushrooms, sliced
15 ml/1 tbsp chopped fresh parsley
salt and freshly ground black pepper
fresh parsley sprigs, to garnish

2 Pour in the stock and bring to the boil. Stir in the red and yellow peppers and reduce the heat. Cook gently for 10 minutes.

3 Add the green beans and mushrooms and continue cooking for a further 10 minutes.

1 Heat the oil in a large frying pan. Add the rice and cook for 2 minutes, until transparent. Add the onion and minced chicken. Cook for 5 minutes, stirring occasionally.

4 Stir in the chopped parsley and season well to taste. Cook for 10 minutes, or until the liquid has been absorbed. Serve immediately, garnished with parsley sprigs.

Risotto with Chicken & Ham

The unique flavour of Parma ham gives a lift to this creamy risotto.

Serves 4

INGREDIENTS
30 ml/2 tbsp olive oil
225 g/8 oz skinless, boneless chicken breast,
   cut into 2.5 cm/1 in cubes
1 onion, finely chopped
1 garlic clove, finely chopped
1.5 ml/¼ tsp saffron strands
50 g/2 oz Parma ham, cut into thin strips
450 g/1 lb/2¼ cups arborio or carnaroli rice
120 ml/4 fl oz/½ cup dry white wine
1.75 litres/3 pints/7½ cups simmering
   chicken stock
25 g/1 oz/2 tbsp butter (optional)
25 g/1 oz/⅓ cup freshly grated Parmesan
   cheese, plus extra shavings to serve
salt and freshly ground black pepper
fresh parsley sprig, to garnish

1 Heat the oil in a medium, heavy-based saucepan, add the chicken and cook, stirring frequently, until it starts to turn white.

2 Reduce the heat and add the onion, garlic, saffron and Parma ham. Cook, stirring, until the onion is soft. Stir in the rice. Sauté for 1–2 minutes, stirring constantly.

3 Add the wine and bring to the boil. Simmer gently until almost all the wine is absorbed. Add the hot stock gradually, following steps 4–5 for Making Risotto. Stir in the butter, if using, and the Parmesan. Season and serve, garnished with parsley and sprinkled with more Parmesan.

Chicken & Bean Risotto

Brown rice adds a delicious nutty taste to this spicy risotto.

Serves 4–6

INGREDIENTS
1 onion, chopped
2 garlic cloves, crushed
1 red chilli, seeded and finely chopped
175 g/6 oz/2½ cups mushrooms, sliced
2 celery sticks, chopped
200 g/7 oz/1 cup longgrain brown rice
450 ml/¾ pint/scant 2 cups simmering
   chicken stock
150 ml/¼ pint/⅔ cup white wine
225 g/8 oz skinless, boneless chicken breast
400 g/14 oz can red kidney beans
200 g/7 oz can sweetcorn kernels
115 g/4 oz/⅔ cup sultanas
175 g/6 oz small broccoli florets
30–45 ml/2–3 tbsp chopped fresh mixed herbs
salt and freshly ground black pepper

1 Put the onion, garlic, chilli, mushrooms, celery, rice, stock and wine in a saucepan. Cover, bring to the boil and simmer over a gentle heat for 15 minutes.

2 Dice the chicken. Add to the rice mixture with the kidney beans, sweetcorn and sultanas. Cook for a further 20 minutes, until almost all the liquid has been absorbed but the mixture is still moist.

3 Meanwhile, cook the broccoli in boiling water or a steamer for 5 minutes, then drain thoroughly. Stir the broccoli into the risotto. Add the chopped fresh herbs, season to taste and serve immediately.

Ham, Pea & Cheese Risotto

This classic risotto is traditionally served as a starter in Italy, but makes an excellent supper dish with a crisp salad.

Serves 4

INGREDIENTS
75 g/3 oz/6 tbsp butter
1 small onion, finely chopped
275 g/10 oz/1½ cups arborio or carnaroli rice
150 ml/¼ pint/⅔ cup dry white wine
about 1 litre/1¾ pints/4 cups simmering
   chicken stock
225 g/8 oz/2 cups frozen petits pois,
   thawed
115 g/4 oz cooked ham, diced
salt and freshly ground black pepper
50 g/2 oz/⅔ cup Parmesan cheese, to serve

3 Gradually add the hot stock, following steps 4–5 for Making Risotto. Add the peas towards the end of the cooking time.

1 Melt 50 g/2 oz/4 tbsp of the butter in a pan, add the onion and cook gently for about 3 minutes, stirring frequently, until softened.

2 Add the rice, stir until the grains are well-coated, then pour in the wine. Stir until it stops sizzling and most of it has been absorbed.

4 Gently stir in the ham and the remaining butter. Heat through until the butter has melted, then season to taste. Transfer to a warmed serving bowl. Grate or shave a little Parmesan over the top and hand the rest around separately.

Smoky Bacon & Tomato Risotto

Plenty of golden onions, smoked bacon and sun-dried tomatoes will make you want to keep going back for more of this dish.

Serves 4

INGREDIENTS
8 sun-dried tomatoes in olive oil
275 g/10 oz good-quality rindless, smoked
    back bacon
75 g/3 oz/6 tbsp butter
450 g/1 lb/2 cups onions, roughly chopped
2 garlic cloves, crushed
350 g/12 oz/scant 1¾ cups arborio or
    carnaroli rice
900 ml/1½ pints/3¾ cups simmering
    vegetable stock
300 ml/½ pint/1¼ cups dry white wine
50 g/2 oz/⅔ cup freshly grated Parmesan cheese
45 ml/3 tbsp mixed chopped fresh chives and
    flatleaf parsley
salt and freshly ground black pepper

2 Heat 15 ml/1 tbsp of the reserved oil in a large saucepan and fry the bacon until golden. Remove and drain on kitchen paper.

3 Add 25 g/1 oz/2 tbsp of the butter to the pan and cook the onions and garlic over a medium heat for 10 minutes, until softened and golden.

4 Stir in the rice and cook for 1 minute, until turning translucent. Mix together the stock and wine and add gradually to the rice, following steps 4–5 for Making Risotto.

5 Just before serving, stir in the bacon, tomatoes, half the Parmesan and herbs, and the remaining butter. Season to taste (remember that the bacon may be quite salty) and serve, sprinkled with the remaining Parmesan and herbs.

1 Drain the sun-dried tomatoes and reserve the oil. Roughly chop the tomatoes and set aside. Cut the smoked bacon into 2.5 cm/1 in strips.

Mushroom & Bacon Risotto

Dried mushrooms bring an extra depth of flavour to this dish, and colourful tomatoes and olives are added just before serving.

Serves 4

INGREDIENTS
30 ml/2 tbsp sunflower oil
1 large onion, chopped
75 g/3 oz smoked bacon, chopped
350 g/12 oz/1¾ cups arborio or carnaroli rice
1–2 garlic cloves, crushed
15 g/½ oz/¼ cup dried sliced mushrooms,
  soaked in a little boiling water
175 g/6 oz/2½ cups mushrooms, sliced
1.2 litres/2 pints/5 cups simmering stock
a few sprigs of fresh oregano or thyme
15 g/½ oz/1 tbsp butter
a little dry white wine
45 ml/3 tbsp chopped, peeled tomato
8–10 black olives, stoned and quartered
salt and freshly ground black pepper
sprigs of fresh thyme, to garnish

1 Heat the oil. Add the onion and bacon and gently cook until the onion is tender.

2 Stir in the rice and garlic and cook over a high heat for 2–3 minutes, until the rice is well coated. Add the dried mushrooms and their liquid, the fresh mushrooms, half the stock, the herb and seasoning. Bring to the boil, reduce the heat to minimum, cover tightly and leave to cook.

3 Check the liquid in the risotto occasionally and add more stock as required, until the rice is cooked, but not mushy. Stir in the butter, wine, tomatoes and olives. Garnish with thyme and serve.

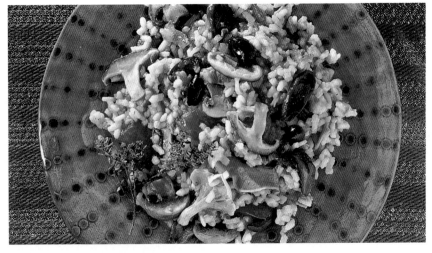

Onion Squash & Bacon Risotto

Squash is an underrated vegetable which marries superbly with
bacon in this tasty risotto.

Serves 4

INGREDIENTS

30 ml/2 tbsp olive oil
1 onion, chopped
1–2 garlic cloves, crushed
115 g/4 oz streaky bacon,
   chopped
1 onion squash or pumpkin, about
   900 g–1 kg/2–2¼ lb, peeled, seeded and
   cut into small chunks
115 g/4 oz/generous ½ cup arborio or
   carnaroli rice
600–750 ml/1–1¼ pints/2½–3 cups
   simmering chicken stock
40 g/1½ oz/generous ⅓ cup freshly grated
   Parmesan cheese, plus extra shavings
15 ml/1 tbsp chopped fresh parsley
salt and freshly ground black pepper

1 Heat the oil and fry the onion and
garlic for about 3–4 minutes,
stirring frequently until beginning to
soften. Add the bacon and continue
frying until both the onion and bacon
are lightly golden.

2 Add the squash or pumpkin and
stir-fry for a few minutes. Add the
rice and stir for about 2 minutes.

3 Gradually add the hot stock and
simmer, stirring frequently,
following steps 4–5 for Making
Risotto. When the rice and squash are
tender, season to taste with salt and
pepper. Stir in the grated Parmesan.
Sprinkle over the parsley and
Parmesan shavings and serve.

Pancetta & Broad Bean Risotto

This delicious risotto makes a healthy and filling meal, served with cooked, fresh, seasonal vegetables or a salad.

Serves 4

INGREDIENTS
15 ml/1 tbsp olive oil
1 onion, chopped
2 garlic cloves, finely chopped
175 g/6 oz smoked pancetta, diced
350 g/12 oz/1¾ cups arborio or
    carnaroli rice
1.2 litres/2 pints/5 cups simmering
    chicken stock
225 g/8 oz frozen baby broad beans
30 ml/2 tbsp chopped fresh mixed herbs,
    such as parsley, thyme and oregano
salt and freshly ground black pepper
chopped fresh flatleaf parsley,
    to garnish
shavings of Parmesan cheese, to serve

2 Add the rice and cook for 1 minute, stirring. Gradually add the hot stock, following steps 4–5 for Making Risotto.

3 Meanwhile, cook the broad beans in a saucepan of lightly salted, boiling water for about 3 minutes. Drain, peel and keep warm.

1 Heat the oil in a large saucepan or casserole dish. Add the onion, garlic and pancetta and cook gently for about 5 minutes, stirring occasionally.

4 When the rice is cooked, stir in the beans, mixed herbs and seasoning. Garnish with parsley and serve sprinkled with shavings of Parmesan.

Pepper & Courgette Risotto with Vermouth

All it takes is a little time and patience to create this superb risotto, flavoured with vermouth and Parmesan.

Serves 4

INGREDIENTS

30 ml/2 tbsp olive oil
1 onion, chopped
2 garlic cloves, crushed
250 g/9 oz/1¼ cups arborio or
   carnaroli rice
1 litre/1¾ pints/4 cups simmering chicken
   or vegetable stock
2 courgettes, chopped
1 green pepper, seeded and chopped
50 g/2 oz/⅔ cups freshly grated
   Parmesan cheese
30 ml/2 tbsp dry white vermouth
salt and freshly ground black pepper
shavings of Parmesan cheese,
   to serve

2 Stir in the rice. Add salt and pepper to taste and cook for 2 minutes. Begin to add the hot stock, following steps 4–5 for Making Risotto.

3 After the first ladleful of stock has been absorbed by the rice, tip the courgettes and pepper into the pan.

1 Heat the oil in a large frying pan. Fry the onion until soft, then add the garlic and continue cooking for 1 minute more.

4 When the rice and vegetables are cooked, stir in the cheese and vermouth. Reheat briefly and serve, topped with Parmesan shavings.

Risotto with Mushrooms

The addition of wild mushrooms gives this risotto a wonderful flavour.

Serves 3–4

INGREDIENTS

25 g/1 oz/½ cup dried wild mushrooms,
    preferably porcini
175 g/6 oz/2½ cups fresh cultivated
    mushrooms, thinly sliced
juice of ½ lemon
75 g/3 oz/6 tbsp butter
30 ml/2 tbsp finely chopped fresh parsley
900 ml/1½ pints/3¾ cups simmering meat,
    chicken or vegetable stock
30 ml/2 tbsp olive oil
1 small onion, finely chopped
275 g/10 oz/1½ cups arborio or carnaroli rice
120 ml/4 fl oz/½ cup dry white wine
45 ml/3 tbsp freshly grated Parmesan cheese
salt and freshly ground black pepper
fresh parsley sprig, to garnish

1 Soak the dried mushrooms in a
small bowl in about 350 ml/
12 fl oz/1½ cups warm water for at
least 40 minutes. Rinse the mushrooms
thoroughly. Filter the soaking water
through a sieve lined with kitchen
paper and reserve.

2 Toss the fresh mushrooms with
the lemon juice. In a large, heavy-
based pan, melt a third of the butter.
Stir in the fresh mushrooms and cook
over moderate heat until they begin
to brown. Add the fresh parsley, cook
for 30 seconds more, then remove
and set aside.

3 Place the stock in a saucepan. Add
the mushroom water and simmer
gently until needed.

4 Heat another third of the butter
with the olive oil in the pan the
mushrooms were cooked in. Stir in
the onion and cook until soft and
golden. Add the rice, stirring for
1–2 minutes to coat the grains. Add
the soaked and sautéed mushrooms
and mix well.

5 Pour in the wine and cook over
moderate heat until it is absorbed.
Gradually add the hot stock, following
steps 4–5 for Making Risotto.

6 Remove the risotto pan from the
heat. Stir in the remaining butter
and the Parmesan. Season to taste.
Allow the risotto to rest for 3–4
minutes before serving, garnished with
the parsley sprig.

Saffron & Gremolata Risotto

This risotto, scattered with cheese and gremolata, makes a delicious light meal or an accompaniment to a meaty stew or casserole.

Serves 4

INGREDIENTS
5 ml/1 tsp (or 1 sachet) saffron strands
25 g/1 oz/2 tbsp butter
1 large onion, finely chopped
275 g/10 oz/1½ cups arborio or
   carnaroli rice
150 ml/¼ pint/⅔ cup dry white wine
1 litre/1¾ pints/4 cups simmering chicken
   or vegetable stock
salt and freshly ground
   black pepper
shavings of Parmesan cheese, to serve

FOR THE GREMOLATA
2 garlic cloves, crushed
60 ml/4 tbsp chopped fresh parsley
finely grated rind of 1 lemon

1 To make the gremolata, mix together the garlic, parsley and lemon rind. Set aside until you are ready to serve the risotto.

2 To make the risotto, put the saffron in a small bowl with 15 ml/1 tbsp boiling water and leave to stand. Melt the butter in a heavy-based saucepan and gently fry the onion for 5 minutes.

3 Stir in the rice and cook for about 2 minutes, until it becomes translucent. Add the wine and saffron mixture and cook for several minutes, until the wine is absorbed.

4 Gradually add the hot stock, stirring frequently, following steps 4–5 for Making Risotto.

5 Season the risotto with salt and pepper and transfer to a serving dish. Scatter lavishly with shavings of Parmesan cheese and the gremolata.

VARIATION: If preferred, stir plenty of grated Parmesan cheese into the risotto.

Parmesan & Saffron Risotto

This classic risotto is traditionally served with osso buco, but makes a delicious first course or light supper dish in its own right.

Serves 4

INGREDIENTS
about 1.2 litres/2 pints/5 cups simmering
    beef, chicken or vegetable stock
good pinch of saffron threads or 1 sachet
    saffron powder
75 g/3 oz/6 tbsp butter
1 onion, finely chopped
275 g/10 oz/1½ cups arborio or carnaroli rice
75 g/3 oz/1 cup freshly grated
    Parmesan cheese
salt and freshly ground black pepper

3 Add the rice. Stir until the grains are well-coated, then stir in the infused saffron and liquid. Gradually add hot stock, following steps 4–5 for Making Risotto.

4 When the rice is cooked, gently stir in about two-thirds of the Parmesan and the remaining butter. Heat through until the butter has melted, then season to taste.

1 Ladle a little of the simmering stock into a small bowl. Sprinkle the saffron threads or powder over the stock and leave to infuse.

2 Melt 50 g/2 oz/4 tbsp of the butter in a large saucepan until foaming. Add the onion and cook gently for about 3 minutes, stirring frequently, until softened.

5 Transfer the risotto to a warmed serving bowl and serve with the remaining Parmesan sprinkled on top and a grinding of black pepper.

VARIATION: This risotto can be made more substantial by adding cubes of a small, peeled and seeded butternut squash with the rice.

Risotto with Spring Vegetables

Yellow courgettes make this one of the prettiest risottos.

Serves 4

INGREDIENTS
150 g/5 oz/generous 1 cup shelled fresh peas
115 g/4 oz/1 cup French beans, cut into
    short lengths
30 ml/2 tbsp olive oil
75 g/3 oz/6 tbsp butter
2 small yellow courgettes, cut
    into matchsticks
1 onion, finely chopped
275 g/10 oz/1½ cups arborio or carnaroli rice
120 ml/4 fl oz/½ cup dry
    white vermouth
about 1 litre/1¾ pints/4 cups simmering
    chicken stock
75 g/3 oz/1 cup freshly grated
    Parmesan cheese
a small handful of fresh basil leaves,
    finely shredded, plus a few whole
    leaves to garnish
salt and freshly ground black pepper

1 Blanch the peas and beans in a
large saucepan of lightly salted
boiling water for 2–3 minutes until
just tender. Drain, refresh under cold
running water, drain again and set
aside for later.

2 Heat the oil and 25 g/1 oz/2 tbsp
of the butter in a medium saucepan
until foaming. Add the courgettes and
cook gently for 2–3 minutes, until just
softened. Remove with a slotted spoon
and set aside.

3 Add the onion to the pan and
cook gently for about 3 minutes,
stirring frequently, until softened.

4 Stir in the rice until the grains start
to swell and burst, then add the
vermouth. Stir until the vermouth has
been absorbed by the rice, then
gradually add the hot stock, following
steps 4–5 for Making Risotto.

5 Gently stir in the vegetables, the
remaining butter and about half the
Parmesan. Heat through, then stir in
the shredded basil and season to taste.
Garnish with a few whole basil leaves
and serve hot, with the remaining
grated Parmesan in a separate bowl.

VARIATIONS: Shelled broad beans
can be used instead of the peas, and
asparagus tips instead of the French
beans. Use green courgettes if
yellow ones are unavailable.

Pumpkin & Pistachio Risotto

You can make this elegant combination of creamy, golden rice, orange pumpkin and pistachio nuts as pale or as vivid as you like by adding different quantities of saffron.

Serves 4

INGREDIENTS
1.2 litres/2 pints/5 cups simmering vegetable
    stock or water
generous pinch of saffron threads
30 ml/2 tbsp olive oil
1 medium onion, chopped
2 garlic cloves, crushed
450 g/1 lb/2¼ cups arborio or carnaroli rice
900 g/2 lb pumpkin, peeled, seeded and cut
    into 2 cm/¾ in cubes
175 ml/6 fl oz/¾ cup dry white wine
15 g/½ oz Parmesan cheese, finely grated
50 g/2 oz/½ cup pistachio nuts
45 ml/3 tbsp chopped fresh marjoram or
    oregano, plus extra leaves to garnish
salt, freshly grated nutmeg and ground
    black pepper

1 Ladle a little of the simmering stock into a small bowl. Add the saffron threads and leave to infuse.

2 Heat the oil in a large saucepan. Add the onion and garlic and cook gently for about 5 minutes, until softened. Add the rice and pumpkin and cook for a few more minutes, until the rice looks transparent.

3 Pour in the wine and allow it to bubble hard. When it is absorbed, add the infused saffron and liquid and begin to add the hot stock, following steps 4–5 for Making Risotto.

4 When the rice and pumpkin are cooked, stir in the grated Parmesan, cover the pan and leave to stand for 5 minutes.

5 Stir in the pistachios and marjoram or oregano. Season to taste with a little salt, nutmeg and pepper. Scatter over a few extra marjoram or oregano leaves and serve.

Leek, Mushroom & Lemon Risotto

A delicious risotto, packed full of flavour, this is a great recipe for an informal supper with friends.

Serves 4

INGREDIENTS
30 ml/2 tbsp olive oil
3 garlic cloves, crushed
225 g/8 oz trimmed leeks, roughly chopped
225 g/8 oz/generous 3 cups chestnut
    mushrooms, roughly chopped
75 g/3 oz/6 tbsp butter
1 large onion, roughly chopped
350 g/12 oz/1¾ cups arborio or carnaroli rice
1.2 litres/2 pints/5 cups simmering
    vegetable stock
grated rind and juice of 1 lemon
50 g/2 oz/⅔ cup freshly grated
    Parmesan cheese
60 ml/4 tbsp mixed chopped fresh chives
    and flatleaf parsley
salt and freshly ground black pepper
lemon wedges, to serve

1 Heat the oil in a large saucepan and cook the garlic for 1 minute. Add the leeks, mushrooms and plenty of seasoning and cook over a medium heat for about 10 minutes, or until softened and browned. Remove from the pan and set aside.

2 Add 25 g/1 oz/2 tbsp of the butter to the pan and cook the onion over a medium heat for about 5 minutes, until softened and golden.

3 Stir in the rice and cook for 1 minute, until the grains are coated in the fat. Gradually add the hot stock, stirring frequently, following steps 4–5 for Making Risotto.

4 Just before serving, stir in the leeks, mushrooms, remaining butter, grated lemon rind and 45ml/3 tbsp of the juice, half the Parmesan and herbs. Allow to warm through, adjust the seasoning and sprinkle with the remaining Parmesan and herbs. Serve with lemon wedges.

Tomato & Cannellini Bean Risotto

Use plum tomatoes in this dish for their fresh, vibrant flavour.

Serves 4

INGREDIENTS

675 g/1½ lb firm ripe tomatoes, preferably
   plum, halved, skinned and seeded
50 g/2 oz/4 tbsp butter
1 onion, finely chopped
275 g/10 oz/1½ cups arborio or
   carnaroli rice
about 1.2 litres/2 pints/5 cups simmering
   vegetable stock
400 g/14 oz can cannellini
   beans, drained
50 g/2 oz/⅔ cup grated Parmesan cheese,
   plus extra, to serve
salt and freshly ground black pepper
10–12 fresh basil leaves, shredded, to serve

1 Sieve the tomato seeds over a bowl, pressing well. Reserve the juice. Dice the tomato flesh.

2 Melt the butter, add the onion and cook for 5 minutes, until beginning to soften. Add the tomatoes, the reserved juice and seasoning, then cook, stirring occasionally, for about 10 minutes.

3 Add the rice and stir to coat. Gradually add the hot stock, following steps 4–5 for Making Risotto. Stir in the beans and Parmesan and heat through. Serve sprinkled with basil and Parmesan.

Mushroom, Leek & Cashew Nut Risotto

Brown rice is used for this flavoursome, nutty vegetable risotto.

Serves 4

INGREDIENTS
225 g/8 oz/generous 1 cup brown rice
900 ml/1½ pints/3¾ cups simmering
    vegetable stock or a mixture of stock and
    dry white wine in the ratio of 5:1
15 ml/1 tbsp walnut or hazelnut oil
2 leeks, sliced
225 g/8 oz/generous 3 cups mixed wild or
    cultivated mushrooms, trimmed and sliced
50 g/2 oz/½ cup cashew nuts
grated rind of 1 lemon
30 ml/2 tbsp chopped fresh thyme
25 g/1 oz/scant ¼ cup pumpkin seeds
salt and freshly ground black pepper
fresh thyme leaves and lemon wedges

1 Place the rice in a saucepan, pour in the stock (or stock and wine) and bring to the boil. Cook gently for about 30 minutes, until the stock has been absorbed and the rice is tender.

2 Heat the oil and fry the vegetables gently for 3–4 minutes. Add the cashew nuts, lemon rind and chopped thyme to the vegetables and cook for 1–2 minutes more. Season.

3 Drain the cooked rice and stir in the vegetables. Turn into a serving dish. Scatter the pumpkin seeds over the top, garnish with thyme and lemon wedges and serve.

Red Pepper Risotto

If you use brown rice for this risotto, reduce the amount of liquid and add it all at the same time for a drier dish with a nutty flavour.

Serves 6

INGREDIENTS
3 large red peppers
30 ml/2 tbsp olive oil
3 large garlic cloves, thinly sliced
1½ x 400 g/14 oz cans chopped
    tomatoes
2 bay leaves
450 g/1 lb/2¼ cups arborio or carnaroli
    or brown rice
1.2–1.5 litres/2–2½ pints/5–6¼ cups
    simmering vegetable stock
6 fresh basil leaves, snipped
salt and freshly ground black pepper

2 Heat the oil in a large saucepan. Add the garlic and tomatoes and cook over a gentle heat for 5 minutes, then add the pepper slices and bay leaves. Stir well and cook for 15 minutes more.

3 Stir the rice into the vegetables and cook for 2 minutes, then gradually add the hot stock, following steps 4–5 for Making Risotto.

4 When the rice is tender, season to taste. Remove the pan from the heat, cover and leave to stand for 10 minutes. Stir in the fresh basil leaves and serve.

1 Preheat the grill. Grill the peppers until the skins are blistered all over. Put them in a bowl, cover with several layers of damp kitchen paper or a layer of cling film and leave for about 10 minutes. Peel off the skins, then slice the peppers, discarding the core and seeds.

VARIATION: 115 g/4 oz/1 cup blanched almonds or cashew nuts could be added at step 3 if desired, for a more filling dish.

Porcini & Parmesan Risotto

For this variation of the classic risotto *alla milanese*, saffron, porcini mushrooms and Parmesan are stirred into the creamy cooked rice.

Serves 4

INGREDIENTS
10 g/¼ oz/2 tbsp dried porcini mushrooms
300 ml/½ pint/1¼ cups warm water
1.2 litres/2 pints/5 cups simmering
    vegetable stock
generous pinch of saffron strands
30 ml/2 tbsp olive oil
1 onion, finely chopped
1 garlic clove, crushed
250 g/9 oz/1¼ cups arborio or carnaroli rice
150 ml/¼ pint/⅔ cup dry white wine or
    45 ml/3 tbsp dry white vermouth
25 g/1 oz/2 tbsp butter
50 g/2 oz/⅔ cup freshly grated
    Parmesan cheese
salt and freshly ground black pepper

1 Soak the dried mushrooms in the warm water for 20 minutes. Lift out with a slotted spoon. Filter the soaking water through a layer of kitchen paper in a sieve, then add it to the simmering stock.

2 Put about 45ml/3 tbsp of the hot stock in a cup and stir in the saffron strands. Set aside.

3 Finely chop the mushrooms. Heat the oil and lightly sauté the onion, garlic and mushrooms for 5 minutes. Gradually add the rice and cook for 2 minutes, stirring. Season.

4 Pour in the wine or vermouth. Cook, stirring, until it has been absorbed. Gradually add the hot stock stirring frequently, following steps 4–5 for Making Risotto.

5 Stir in the butter, saffron water and strands and half the grated Parmesan. Serve, sprinkled with the remaining Parmesan.

COOK'S TIP: Pecorino makes a delicious alternative to Parmesan in this risotto.

Lentil Risotto with Vegetables

In this dish brown basmati rice is cooked with lentils and colourful fresh vegetables are stirred in at the end of the cooking time.

Serves 4

INGREDIENTS
45 ml/3 tbsp sunflower oil
1 large onion, thinly sliced
2 garlic cloves, crushed
1 large carrot, cut into matchsticks
225 g/8 oz/generous 1 cup
    brown basmati rice, washed
    and drained
115 g/4 oz/½ cup green or brown lentils,
    soaked overnight and drained
5 ml/1 tsp ground cumin
5 ml/1 tsp ground cinnamon
20 black cardamom seeds
6 cloves
600 ml/1 pint/2½ cups simmering
    vegetable stock
2 celery sticks, thinly sliced
1 large avocado, peeled, stoned and diced
3 plum tomatoes, diced
salt and freshly ground black pepper
green salad, to serve

1 Heat the oil in a wide pan and gently fry the onion, garlic and carrot for 5–6 minutes, until the onion is transparent and the carrot is slightly softened.

2 Add the drained rice and lentils together with the cumin, cinnamon, cardamom seeds and cloves and continue frying over a low heat for a further 5 minutes, stirring well to prevent sticking.

3 Add the stock and bring to the boil, then cover the pan and simmer very gently for a further 15 minutes, or until the liquid has been absorbed and the rice and lentils are tender. The mixture should still be quite moist. Season to taste.

4 Add the celery, avocado and tomatoes to the rice and lentil mixture, and stir gently to mix. Spoon the risotto into a large serving bowl and serve immediately with a green salad.

VARIATION: Other seasonal vegetables could be used for this risotto. In the summer try diced green or yellow courgettes, aubergine or sweet red pepper. Winter options could include pumpkin, broccoli or leeks.

Creamy Risotto with Asparagus

Asparagus tastes so wonderful cooked like this that it seems to have been invented for the purpose.

Serves 4

INGREDIENTS
30 ml/2 tbsp olive oil
1 onion, finely chopped
2 garlic cloves, crushed
225 g/8 oz/generous 1 cup arborio or
    carnaroli rice
150 ml/¼ pint/⅔ cup white wine
1.5 litres/2½ pints/6¼ cups simmering
    vegetable stock
225 g/8 oz asparagus spears, cut into 2.5 cm/1 in
    pieces, stalks separated from the tips
50 g/2 oz/4 tbsp butter
45ml/3 tbsp freshly grated
    Parmesan cheese
salt and freshly ground black pepper

1 In a large heavy-based saucepan, heat the olive oil and fry the onion and garlic for 10 minutes, until softened but not coloured. Add the rice, stir to coat the grains in oil, and cook for 2–3 minutes. Pour in the white wine and cook over a moderate heat, stirring continuously until absorbed.

2 Begin gradually to add the hot stock, following steps 4–5 for Making Risotto. After about 10 minutes add the chopped asparagus stalks. After another 5 minutes add the asparagus tips to ensure even cooking.

3 When the rice and asparagus are tender but still *al dente*, stir in the butter and Parmesan. Remove from the heat, cover and leave for 2 minutes, then serve.

Risotto-stuffed Aubergines with Spicy Tomato Sauce

Risotto can be used to make a tasty stuffing for vegetables such as aubergines.

Serves 4

INGREDIENTS
4 small aubergines
105 ml/7 tbsp olive oil
1 small onion, chopped
175 g/6 oz/scant 1 cup arborio or
    carnaroli rice
750 ml/1¼ pints/3 cups vegetable stock
15 ml/1 tbsp white wine vinegar
8 fresh basil sprigs, to garnish

FOR THE SAUCE
300 ml/½ pint/1¼ cups thick passata
5 ml/1 tsp mild curry paste
pinch of salt

FOR THE TOPPING
25 g/1 oz/⅓ cup freshly grated
    Parmesan cheese
15 ml/1 tbsp pine nut

1 Preheat the oven to 200°C/400°F/
Gas 6. Cut the aubergines in half
lengthways and cut out the flesh.
Brush the skins with 30 ml/2 tbsp of
the oil, and cook on a baking sheet for
6–8 minutes.

2 Chop the reserved aubergine flesh
and heat the remainder of the olive
oil in a saucepan. Add the aubergine
flesh and the onion and cook gently
for 4 minutes, until soft.

3 Add the rice, stir in the stock and
simmer, uncovered, for 15 minutes.
Stir in the vinegar.

4 Increase the oven temperature to
230°C/450°F/Gas 8. Spoon the
rice mixture into the aubergine
skins, top with cheese and pine
nuts, return to the oven and brown
for 5 minutes.

5 To make the sauce, combine the
passata with the curry paste in a
pan, heat through and add salt to taste.

6 Spoon the sauce on to four large serving plates and position two aubergine halves on each. Garnish with basil sprigs and serve.

COOK'S TIP: There is no need to salt and drain aubergines as they are produced without bitter juices.

Lemon & Herb Risotto Cake

This unusual rice dish can be served as a main course with salad, or as a satisfying side dish. It's also good served cold, and packs well for picnics.

Serves 4

INGREDIENTS
1 small leek, thinly sliced
600 ml/1 pint/2½ cups simmering chicken stock
225 g/8 oz/1 cup arborio or carnaroli rice
finely grated rind of 1 lemon
30 ml/2 tbsp chopped fresh chives
30 ml/2 tbsp chopped fresh parsley
75 g/3 oz/¾ cup grated Mozzarella cheese
salt and freshly ground black pepper
fresh parsley sprigs and lemon wedges,
    to garnish

1 Preheat the oven to 200°C/400°F/ Gas 6. Lightly oil a 21 cm/8½ in round, loose-bottomed cake tin.

2 Cook the leek in a large pan with 45ml/3 tbsp of the stock, stirring over a moderate heat, to soften. Add the rice and the remaining stock.

3 Bring to the boil. Cover the pan and simmer gently, stirring occasionally, for about 20 minutes, or until all the liquid is absorbed.

4 Stir in the lemon rind, herbs, cheese and seasoning. Spoon into the tin, cover with foil and bake for 30–35 minutes, or until lightly browned. Turn out and serve in slices, garnished with parsley sprigs and lemon wedges.

COOK'S TIP: If this dish is being made for a picnic, it is best eaten on the day of preparation as cooked rice will not keep for more than 24 hours.

Timbale of Rice with Ham & Peas

The *timbale* is so named because it looks like an inverted kettledrum.

Serves 4

INGREDIENTS
75 g/3 oz/6 tbsp butter
30 ml/2 tbsp olive oil
1 small onion, finely chopped
50 g/2 oz/⅓ cup ham, cut into small dice
45 ml/3 tbsp finely chopped fresh parsley
2 garlic cloves, very finely chopped
225 g/8 oz/2 cups shelled peas, fresh or
    frozen and thawed
60 ml/4 tbsp water
275 g/10 oz/1½ cups arborio or carnaroli rice
1.2 litres/2 pints/5 cups simmering meat or
    vegetable stock
75 g/3 oz/1 cup freshly grated
    Parmesan cheese
175 g/6 oz/¾ cup Fontina cheese, sliced
salt and freshly ground black pepper
fresh parsley sprig, to garnish

1 Heat half the butter and all the oil in a large, frying pan. Add the onion and cook until it softens. Add the ham and stir for 3–4 minutes. Stir in the chopped parsley and garlic.

2 Cook for 2 minutes. Add the peas, mix well, season and add the water. Cover the pan and cook for 8 minutes for fresh peas, 4 minutes for frozen peas. Remove the lid and cook until all the liquid has evaporated. Transfer half the pea mixture to a dish and set aside.

3 Butter a flat-bottomed ovenproof dish and line the bottom with a round of buttered greaseproof paper.

4 Stir the rice into the pea mixture in the pan. After 1–2 minutes, begin to add the hot stock gradually, stirring frequently, following steps 4–5 for Making Risotto.

5 Preheat the oven to 180°C/350°F/ Gas 4. When the rice is tender, adjust the seasoning and stir in most of the remaining butter and half the grated Parmesan.

6 Sprinkle a little Parmesan into the bottom of the dish. Spoon half the rice into the dish. Then a layer of the Fontina slices and a layer of reserved cooked peas and ham. Sprinkle with Parmesan.

7 Cover with the remaining Fontina slices and end with the rice. Sprinkle with Parmesan and dot with butter. Bake in the oven for 15 minutes. Remove from the oven and allow to stand for 10 minutes.

8 To unmould, slip a knife between the rice and the dish and invert on to a plate. Tap the bottom so that the rice will drop. Remove the paper. Garnish with parsley and serve in wedges.

Green & Orange Risotto

This colourful risotto looks stunning served in cooked squash halves.

Serves 4

INGREDIENTS

40 g/1½ oz/3 tbsp butter or margarine
1 small onion, chopped
50 g/2 oz peeled and coarsely grated acorn
    squash or pumpkin
250 g/9 oz/1¼ cups arborio or
    carnaroli rice
1.2 litres/2 pints/5 cups simmering
    chicken stock
1 courgette, quartered lengthways
    and chopped
150 g/5 oz/1¼ cups frozen peas, thawed
40 g/1½ oz/½ cup freshly grated
    Parmesan cheese
salt and freshly ground black pepper
cooked acorn squash halves, hollowed out,
    to serve (optional)

2 Add the rice and stir to coat all the grains well. Cook for 1 minute over moderate heat, stirring.

3 Begin to add the hot stock gradually, following steps 4–5 for Making Risotto. After about 5 minutes, stir in the courgette pieces. After about 10 minutes, stir in the peas.

1 Melt one-third of the butter or margarine in a heavy saucepan or casserole. Add the onion and cook for about 5 minutes, until softened. Add the grated squash or pumpkin and cook for 1 minute, stirring.

4 When the rice and vegetables are tender, remove the pan from the heat. Add the remaining butter or margarine and the Parmesan and stir well. Season to taste. If you like, serve in hollowed-out acorn squash halves.

Index

First published in 1999 by Lorenz Books © Anness Publishing Limited 1999

Lorenz Books is an imprint of Anness Publishing Limited, Hermes House,
88-89 Blackfriars Road, London SE1 8HA

This edition distributed in Canada by Raincoast Books, 8680 Cambie Street,
Vancouver, British Columbia, V6P 6M9

ISBN 0 7548 0145 4

A CIP catalogue record for this book
is available from the British Library.

Publisher: Joanna Lorenz
Editor: Valerie Ferguson
Series Designer: Bobbie Colgate Stone
Designer: Andrew Heath
Editorial Reader: Marion Wilson
Production Controller: Joanna King

Recipes contributed by: Alex Barker, Michelle
Berriedale-Johnson, Angela Boggiano, Janet Brinkworth,
Carla Capalbo, Frances Cleary, Roz Denny,
Patrizia Diemling, Sarah Edmonds, Joanna Farrow,
Christine France, Shirley Gill, Christine Ingram, Peter Jordan,
Norma MacMillan, Norma Miller, Annie Nichols,
Maggie Pannell, Anne Sheasby, Jenny Stacey,
Steven Wheeler, JeniWright

Photography: William Adams-Lingwood, Karl Adamson,
Steve Baxter, James Duncan, Michelle Garrett,
John Heseltine, Amanda Heywood, Janine Hosegood,
David Jordan, Patrick McLeavey, Thomas Odulate

1 3 5 7 9 10 8 6 4 2

Notes:
For all recipes, quantities are given in both metric and
imperial measures and, where appropriate, measures
are also given in standard cups and spoons.
Follow one set, but not a mixture, because they are
not interchangeable.

Standard spoon and cup measures are level.

1 tsp = 5 ml   1 tbsp =15 ml

1 cup = 250 ml/8 fl oz

Australian standard tablespoons are 20 ml.
Australian readers should use 3 tsp in place of 1 tbsp
for measuring small quantities of gelatine, cornflour,
salt, etc.

Medium eggs are used unless otherwise stated.

Printed in Singapore